INFANT MASSAGE
FROM HEAD TO TOE FOR PARENTS & CAREGIVERS

A STEP-BY-STEP GUIDE

by Alicia J. Jackson

Infant Massage from Head to Toe for Parents and Caregivers; A Step-by-Step Guide

Copyright © 2024 by Alicia J. Jackson

Edited by Oller Publishing & Co.

Cover and Layout Design by Glori Alexander

All rights reserved. No part of this book may be reproduced or used in any manner without the prior written permission of the copyright owner, except for the use of brief quotations in a book review.

ISBN: 978-1-957619-12-5

DEDICATION

First, I would like to dedicate this book to my Lord
and Savior Jesus Christ.
I give Him all the praise and glory!

Second, to my parents,
Bonnie and Jerry Howell, who have loved and supported me
every day of my life. Thank you for always believing in me
and having continued faith in me!

Third, to my beautiful daughter,
Emily Caroline. Emily, you are the love of my life. You have
grown into a very beautiful young lady and you inspire
me every day. Thank you for being a wonderful mother to
Carolina. I am truly blessed to have you as my daughter.

And last, but not least to my beautiful granddaughter,
Carolina Louise.
MeeMommy loves you so much. You have blessed me
abundantly with your beautiful spirit and soul. May God
bless you and keep you all the days of your life.

Love and Blessings,

Alicia Jackson

IMPORTANT NOTICE

This book is written by a Licensed Massage Therapist and Certified Infant Massage Therapist/Instructor. All advice and techniques demonstrated in this book are recommended by a licensed professional.

The ideas, procedures, and suggestions contained in the booklet are not intended as a substitute for consulting with your physician. All matters regarding your child's health requires medical supervision.

Always seek the advice of a trained health professional with any questions you may have regarding a medical condition and before beginning a massage. Proper medical attention should always be sought for specific ailments, as massage is intended to be a supplemental, holistic treatment.

*Front cover is my daughter Emily giving her daughter, Carolina, her first infant massage in the hospital, while I am teaching Emily.

INTRODUCTION

I have always had a heart's desire to perform massage therapy, and I have been a licensed massage therapist and certified infant massage therapist/instructor since 2007. I have also been a licensed medical aesthetician (skin care specialist) since 2002. I first heard about infant massage while attending massage therapy school; so, I researched it, prayed about it, and God led me to practice it.

I worked for a local women's hospital from 2008 through 2020, which was very rewarding because I was helping women feel better during their prenatal and postnatal stages of pregnancy. I have always been a multitasker. I performed in-hospital as well as outpatient massages for patients. I was the instructor for the Infant Massage class, and I offered laser skin care services.

In October 2020, I opened my own private practice, Holistic Health Practitioner OKC. I am still providing massage therapy for women, infants as well as laser skin care. I have truly been blessed with my work, gifts, and talents.

I am a proud mother to one beautiful daughter, Emily, and precious granddaughter, Carolina. I often teach parents things I wish I knew when Emily was a newborn. I loved teaching Emily how to give Carolina infant massages!

If there is one thing I hope all parents and caregivers take away from this book, it is the tummy massage. It usually takes the newborn tummy six to twenty weeks of life to figure out the flow of the colon, but by implementing tummy massage, you can hopefully lessen any digestive issues early on, making both you and your baby much happier.

I hope you find this book useful and informative! Even though infant massage is recommended for babies from birth to twelve months, you can massage your baby for as long as he or she permits as they grow, and it remains helpful.

-Alicia Jackson
Licensed Massage Therapist
Certified Infant Massage Instructor

THINGS TO KNOW ABOUT INFANT MASSAGE

PURPOSE

The purpose of infant massage is to promote healthy, loving touch. Since *touch* is one of the most developed senses at birth, your newborn baby's *lifeline* is *touch*. The more you offer healthy, loving touch, the more your baby will thrive. Infant massage provides important tactile stimulation as well as relaxation and regulation of the respiratory, circulatory, and digestive systems. The soothing effects of infant massage help to ease a gassy tummy and can be very beneficial for your baby. A healthy, loving touch is good for everyone but especially for infants, who are new to the world and need reassurance from someone special.

BENEFITS

Benefits of infant massage for the infant include:

- Promotes a loving, secure, bonded relationship.
- Massage is relaxing, calming, and soothing.
- Helps regulate digestive system and may also reduce gas, colic, and constipation.
- May increase weight gain.
- Decreases stress hormones (cortisol).

The key to a *"Happy Baby"* is a *"Happy Tummy!"* When your baby has a happy tummy:

- Feeding times are more scheduled.
- You will both experience longer sleep patterns. If your baby is sleeping longer, parents and caregivers will have longer sleep time. Mom, if you are sleeping more, your hormones will become more balanced.
- It improves baby's immune system.

Benefits of massage for the massage giver include:

- A loving, secure, and bonded time with the infant.
- Improved parent/caregiver communication and teaches to respond to baby's nonverbal cues.
- Improved understanding of each other, increases confidence and handling skills.

Massage therapy can trigger many physiological changes that help infants and children develop.

Additional benefits include learning to communicate together through:

- Eye contact
- Saying your baby's name
- Saying, "I love you."
- Singing to your baby

These four are strongly encouraged throughout the massage.

WHO SHOULD LEARN HOW TO GIVE INFANT MASSAGE?

The practice of infant massage dates back to ancient times. It is a physical experience of quality time between the parents/caregivers and the child as well as other significant others in the baby's life. Obviously, parents and caregivers should learn how to offer infant massage but others may include grandparents and guardians.

UNDERSTANDING YOUR BABY

Each baby has his or her own unique way of communicating and you will find it easier to take care of your baby when you can understand what your baby is trying to communicate to you in the various stages between sleep and activity. Understanding your baby's behavior will help you get to know your baby better and know the best time to feed your baby, play with them, and when the best time to offer them a massage!

Knowing the subtle variations between asleep and awake in your baby is critical to determining the times to offer infant massage.

Below are descriptions of the most common infant states and cues to help you understand your baby.

- *Quiet Sleep:* Baby will lie still, with no eye movements and will have smooth breathing patterns. He or she will be very hard to wake up.
- *Active Sleep:* Baby will experience some body and facial movements. The eyelids may flutter. This may be your baby's dream state.
- *Drowsy:* Baby's eyes may open and close. They are heavy lidded and glazed. This state occurs just before falling asleep.
- *Quiet Alert:* Baby is awake, alert, and may take a gazing or staring interest in things nearby, making cooing sounds. This is the *Best* time to offer infant massage; the key is to go slowly and allow your baby to relax.
- *Active Sleep:* Baby makes more body movements, is sensitive to noise, and might be hungry. Ask yourself; Is my baby hungry? Does he or she need a diaper change or need a nap? If you answered yes to any of these questions, then this is not a recommended time to begin infant massage.
- *Crying:* Baby will cry, grimace, and make a lot of body movement.

Crying means your baby needs to be soothed with movements like rocking, swaying, or bouncing.

INFANT CUES AND BEHAVIORS

Engagement and disengagement cues are your baby's way of communicating with you what he or she wants. Most of these cues are nonverbal in the early months of life, but knowing about these cues, will make it much easier and more enjoyable to provide care for your baby, offering an infant massage.

- *Engagement* means your baby wants to be held and will be attracted to you. Baby will reach out to you, smiling, cooing, and making eye contact. Their excitement will be apparent with waving arms and legs.
- *Disengagement* means your baby wants to withdraw from being with you. Baby will turn his or her head away and might start crying. Fussiness or pulling away means baby is overwhelmed and needs a break from interaction.

THE MOST COMMONLY MISSED CUE, ESPECIALLY IN NEWBORNS:

Hungry vs. gassy; Always ask yourself, *when was baby's last feeding? Could they be hungry? Gassy?*

WHEN IS A GOOD TIME TO GIVE INFANT MASSAGE?

To offer infant massage does not mean you have to give a full body massage every time. You can choose to just do a quick tummy massage or soothe your baby with a short back massage. The choice is yours. The infant state of *quiet alert* is the best time to offer infant massage. Other times for infant massage are early in the morning, after bath time, or just before bedtime. You will learn when the best time should be by your baby's response. Infant massage is unique to each parent or caregiver, and it is important to follow your baby's likes and dislikes. Holding your baby and applying massage will create a sense of security and a loving bond that you will learn over time what your baby prefers.

Here are some basic guidelines to get you started:

1. **Do not** massage your baby immediately after feeding or when your baby is hungry. Wait thirty to forty-five minutes after feedings to perform a full body massage.
2. **Do not** massage your baby if he or she has a fever.
3. **Do not** massage your baby if *You* are tired, stressed, rushed, or angry. This is not a good time because your baby will sense this from you and the baby will become stressed.

DO YOU NEED TO ASK PERMISSION?

Yes! It is just as if you are asking if your baby is hungry or wants to play. Parents or caregivers need to ask permission for anything they do with their children, especially massage. This gives your baby a chance to express his or her feelings and emotions. Prior to beginning the massage, ask your baby for permission to give him or her a massage.

- Make eye contact with him or her, and ask, "Do you want a massage?" Or "Are you ready for a massage?"
- Watch your baby's body language to know whether he or she is engaging or disengaging. Example: look for a smile on your baby's face or crying.

WHERE IS A SAFE PLACE TO PROVIDE INFANT MASSAGE?

The safest place to provide a full body infant massage is on the floor. Make a pallet with blankets, quilts, and provide two pillows: one for you to sit on and one to support your back. Keeping your back straight, bend forward at your hips, stretching your legs out in front of you. With your legs apart, you can work with the baby between your legs. You may even choose to prop your baby up on a pillow to create a more upright position. Or you can sit on your knees and work with the baby in front of you. If you choose to massage with your baby's diaper off, you will need to place a thick towel under your baby.

WHAT SHOULD THE ENVIRONMENT BE LIKE?

- **Temperature:** Make sure the room you are massaging in is warm. Babies are not good at regulating their body temperature. Use a blanket to swaddle your infant if he or she gets cold.
- **Light:** It is best for the room not to be too bright. Use a lamp, nightlight, or lower your lights if you have a dimmer switch.
- **Music:** Incorporate soothing massage music, lullabies, and heartbeat sounds, which can all add to relaxation.

HOW LONG SHOULD YOU EXPECT THE MASSAGE TO LAST?

Depending on the time you have available, a full body infant massage could last twenty to thirty minutes. Rushing or trying to fit a massage in between other activities may unsettle your baby. If your baby does not engage or show any kind of relaxing emotion, or even if your baby starts crying, the massage is over. You cannot force your baby to relax. Try again when the baby is more receptive. Pick up your baby and give him or her a hug. Comfort your baby and let them know it is okay.

- Remember, during the tummy massage your baby may cry and fuss if he or she is gassy or has constipation.
- Follow your baby's cues! Massage is supposed to be enjoyable for both of you.

MASSAGE TECHNIQUES

These techniques should be performed slowly and smoothly to avoid overstraining the muscles.
- It is advisable to massage on an empty stomach. Use an elevated position if the baby has been diagnosed with gastroesophageal reflux.

- A newborn may hold tension in the abdomen. Do not be surprised if your baby cries or gets uncomfortable during the tummy massage. Picking up your baby during the tummy massage and burping may help.
- It is okay if your baby falls asleep during the massage. It means your baby is relaxed. Some babies do not like to be touched while they are asleep; if this is the case for your baby, then it will be best to continue the massage at another time.
- There is not a correct or incorrect place to start infant massage, or any massage for that matter, but you want it to flow from feet to head or head to toes. Personally, I like starting at the feet and ending on the back (which is the recommended flow of this book, but you could do it in reverse order if you wish.)
- No matter where you start, you always want to have continuous touch. For example, when kneading up the leg, then you want to glide back down rather than kneading up the leg and taking your hand off, and then starting at the ankle again. This gives the baby a constant flow of energy.

SHOULD YOU USE LOTIONS OR OILS?

You may or may not want to use massage oils or lotions on your baby. It is not required. You can give a massage with clothes on or off. Remember, babies cannot regulate their body temperature when they are uncovered. Make sure you keep the room warm.

- Allergy testing should be done with any new product(s) you want to use on your baby. Your baby's skin is very sensitive. To be safe, place a small amount of oil or lotion on the inside of your baby's wrist. Wait twenty to thirty minutes. Check for any redness or a rash that might indicate a reaction.
- Avoid using any nut oils because your baby could have an allergic reaction.
- Choose an unscented oil, which lets your baby bond with your natural scent first.

- Natural or organic oils (carrier oils) such as grapeseed, apricot, safflower, and jojoba work well. You can find these carrier oils at local health food stores or online.

HOW MUCH PRESSURE SHOULD YOU USE?

You are actually going to use some pressure and move the skin. Massage strokes should be a medium yet gentle pressure. Medium pressure will be reassuring to your baby. Watch for any redness on the baby; it can indicate that you might need to lighten your touch. However, too light of touch can be ticklish and aggravating which will not produce relaxation. Massage strokes are usually long, slow, and rhythmic.

MAKE IT UNIQUE

This is your own unique infant massage. Over time you will find your favorite massage strokes and songs to accompany them. Just saying, "I love you" and your familiar touch will make this a unique experience for you and your baby. As your child grows, the massage will grow with them.

LEGS AND FEET

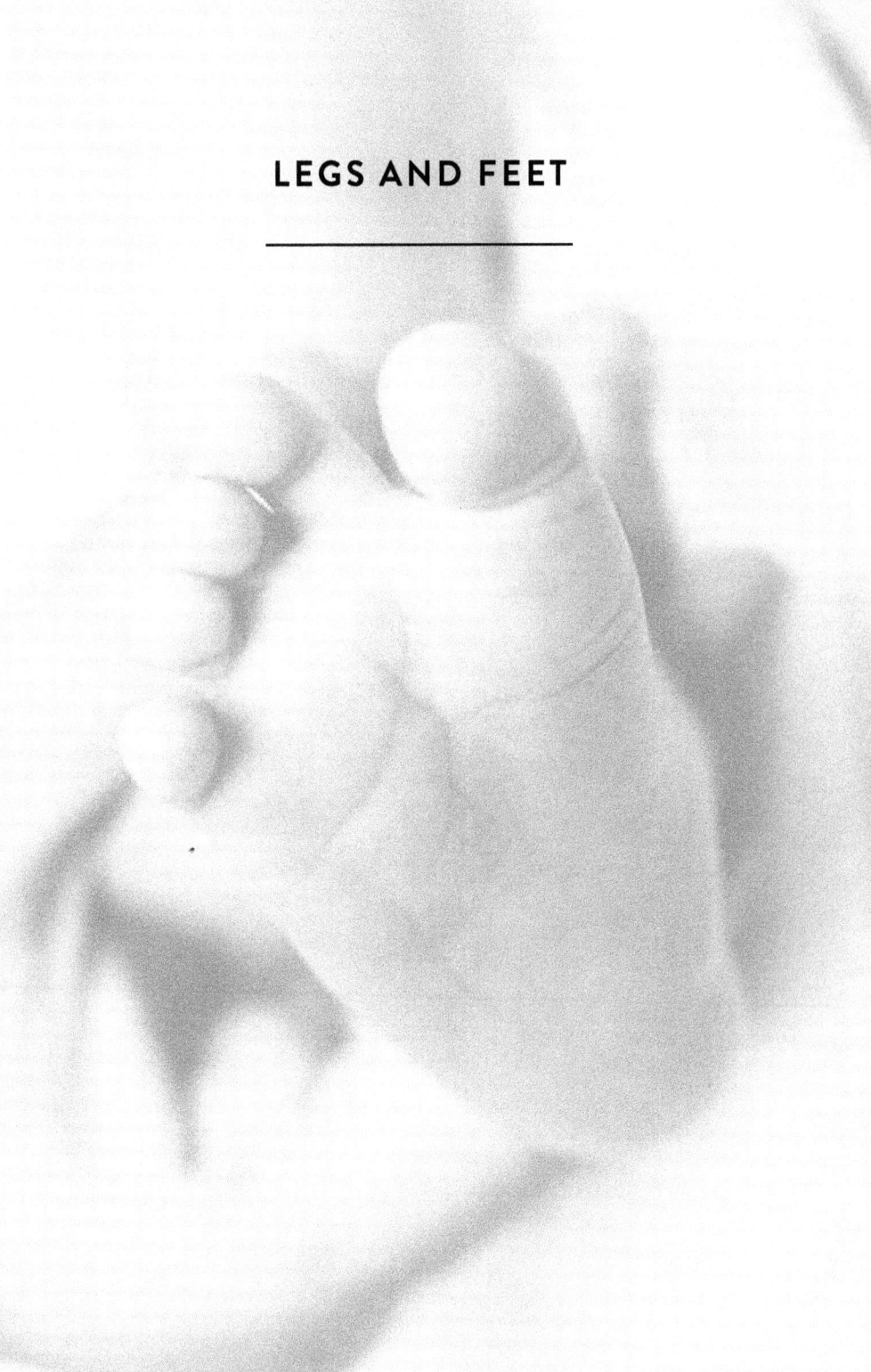

Getting started: Choose either the right or left leg. Do the following massage strokes on one leg and then switch to the other leg and repeat the steps.

Repeat each of the massage strokes three times each.

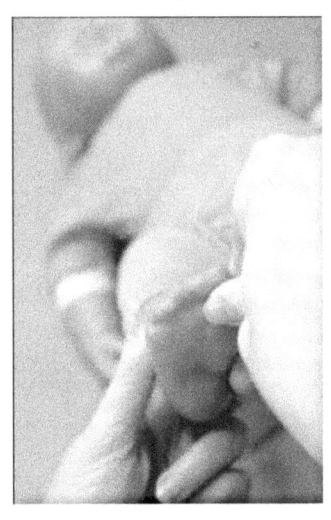

1. **Gently Massage Each Toe:**
   Support the foot at the ankle with one hand; then, using your fingers of your other hand, gently massage by rubbing each toe in a circular motion, using medium pressure, in case your baby is ticklish.

   If your baby seems to be ticklish, gently press each toe and rotate through each toe, starting with the big toe. Make sure to have good eye contact. You can also sing the nursery rhyme, "This Little Piggy Went to Market."

   _____

   _____

   _____

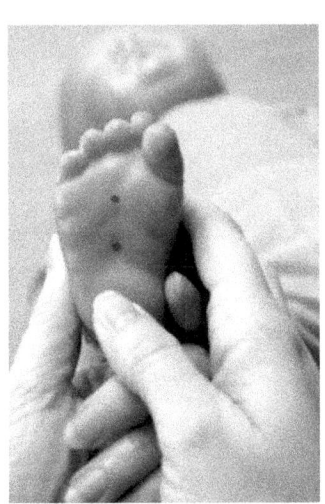

2. **Pressing Through the Bottom of the Foot:**
   Using your thumb, press under the toes, the arch of the foot, and the heel. Apply medium pressure vs. light pressure in case your baby is ticklish.

   _____

   _____

   _____

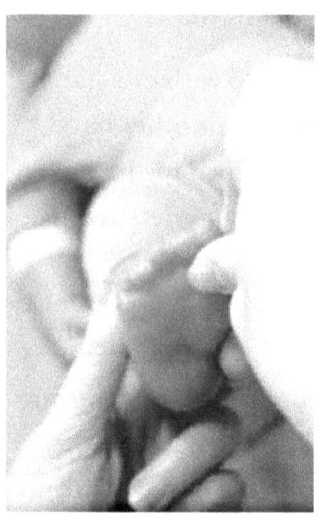

3. Rotating the Ankle:

Support the foot at the ankle with one hand, and then using your other hand, rotate the ankle to the right three times then to the left three times.

_____

_____

_____

4. Stretch the foot down in a plantar flexion:

Gently stretch the foot down.

_____

_____

_____

5. **Stretch the foot in dorsal flexion (up):**
   To stretch the Achilles tendon, rotating the ankle helps to stretch all the ligaments and tendons of the foot and ankle.

   _____

   _____

   _____

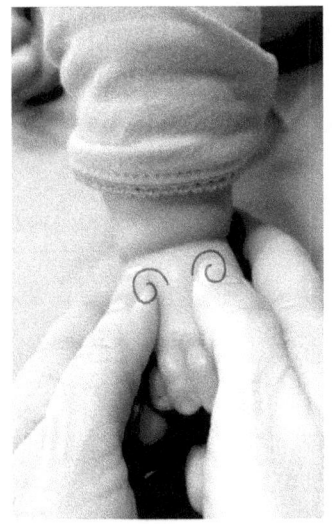

6. **Circular massage on top of the foot:**
   Using both of your thumbs, apply circular massage on top of the foot. Applying small circular motion. This helps promote good circulation and blood flow.

   _____

   _____

   _____

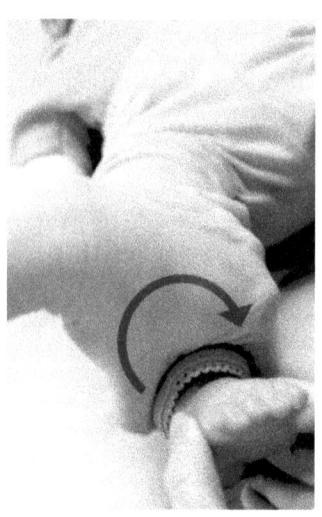

7. Effleurage to the leg:

This is a gliding stroke, long and smooth. Support the foot with one hand and then using the other hand starting at the outside of the ankle, make a "C" shape with your hand.

_____

_____

_____

8. Using medium pressure,

Roll your "C" cupped hand in to the inner ankle and glide up the inner thigh.

_____

_____

_____

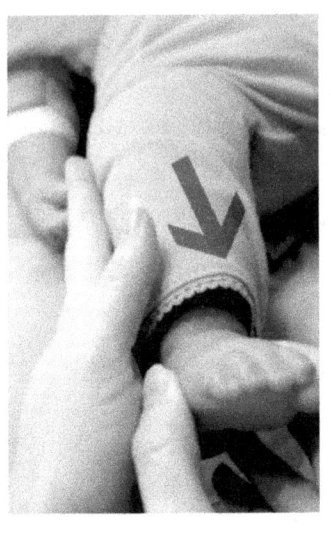

9. Continuing with your "C" cupped hand, glide out to the outer thigh and glide back down to the ankle. *Note:* You can also knead the leg in a circular motion.

Starting at the ankle, begin kneading up the leg (like kneading dough) and gliding back down the leg.

_____

_____

_____

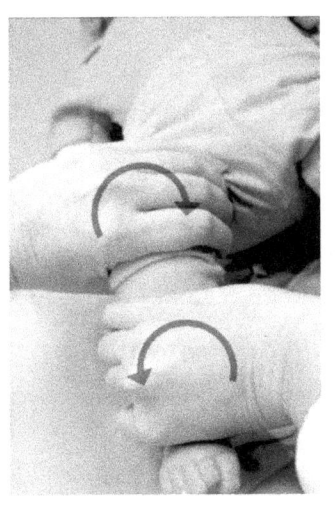

10. Wringing the Leg:
    Place one hand on the upper thigh and your other hand on the lower leg. Wrapping your hands around the leg, use gentle pressure and twist your hands in opposite directions.
    Use a gentle wringing motion back and forth. This motion is like wringing out a washcloth.

_____

_____

_____

11. **Fulling the leg:**
Fulling is a kneading technique in which the tissue is grasped and gently spread out, start at the upper thigh. Place your thumbs in the middle of the upper thigh and press outward. Work down the thigh making three horizontal rows.

_____

_____

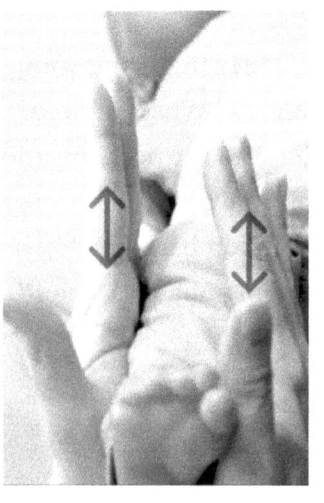

12. **Rolling the Muscles of the Leg:**
Like playing with Play-doh or Silly Putty, place your hands at mid-leg on each side, and gently roll the leg like you are making the Play-Doh into a shape. This is a very gentle rolling action with not a lot of pressure. Note: If you are twisting the knee, you are using too much pressure or rolling action.

_____

_____

_____

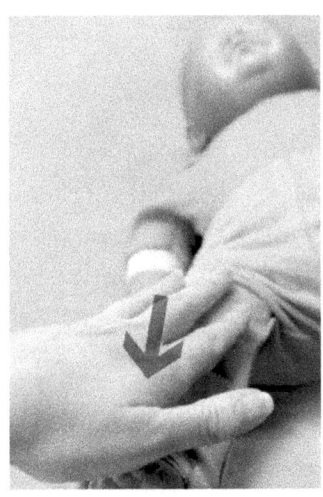

13. Feathering Down the Leg:

Imagine your hand as a feather. Gently use a soft, featherlike stroke and move downward from the upper leg to the ankle.

_____

_____

_____

TUMMY MASSAGE

Getting started: Remember, the key to a "Happy Baby" is a "Happy Tummy!" Tummy massage is going to help reduce gas and constipation. Your baby will then have better feeding schedules, sleep longer and should be happier.

In the first six to twenty weeks, parents have a tendency to feed their babies frequently, or even overfeed, when they see their babies sucking. Parents and caregivers often think the baby is hungry, but this is not always the case. Sucking offers temporary pain relief. If your baby is gassy or colicky, he or she might want to suck on a pacifier or fingers. The baby is using this as a calming and soothing tool. Always make sure you are allowing your baby's tummy time to digest.

Always remember to burp your baby, all day, every day, especially the first six to twenty weeks of life. Your baby needs help moving the gas or air bubbles up or down. Make sure you are using a firm burping technique. Love pats are not burping!

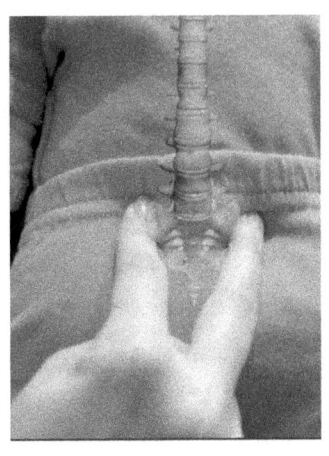

1. **Sacral Release:**

    At the lower spine, there are two dimpled indentions. Holding your baby in an upright position and using your index finger and middle finger, apply gentle pressure in the dimples. When gentle pressure is used on the sacrum, it triggers a sacral release. Sacral release relaxes the digestive system, allowing gas and waste to move through the digestive area without it feeling like a spastic colon would feel to us.

Note: Rocking, swaying, and bouncing relaxes the central nervous system. Add any of these when holding your baby. It takes three to five minutes for the central nervous system to relax. This can be combined with sacral release and burping. It is very calming and soothing.

___

___

___

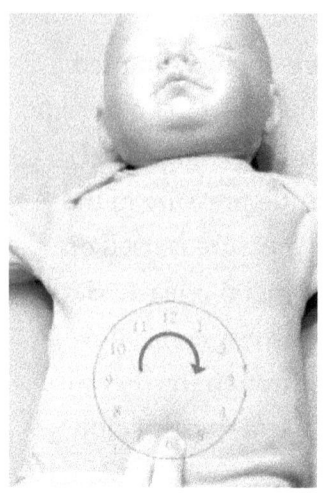

2. **Clockwise Around the Clock:**
Picture a clock sitting on your baby's tummy. The diaphragm is the twelve on the clock and just below the navel is the six on the clock. On the right side going up is the ascending colon; going across the top is the transverse colon; going down on the left is the descending colon. Place your index and middle finger on the twelve (diaphragm) and apply circular massage around the clock (clockwise). This is how the colon flows. When you massage the tummy clockwise, you are helping the colon empty.

Note: understanding that everything empties on our left side (meaning bodily fluids) will help you understand the importance of providing tummy massage. Laying your baby on their left side will allow gravity to move everything from the right side to the left side.

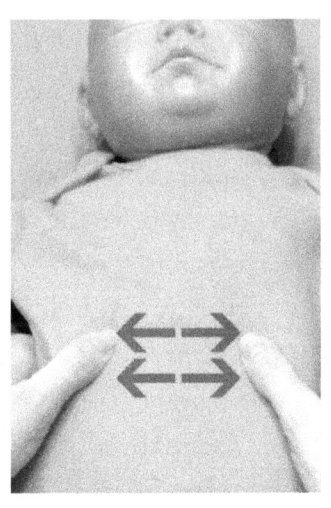

3. Fulling the Tummy:

Place your thumbs at the midline just below the baby's diaphragm. With your thumbs spreading outward to the baby's sides, make two rows, stopping just above the navel. Use a medium pressure. If your baby is gassy or constipated, you may want to apply a firmer pressure.

_____

_____

_____

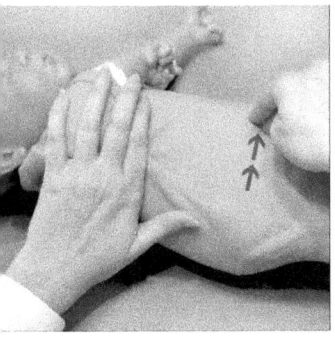

4. Let Your Fingers Do the Walking:

Lay your baby on his or her left side. From the baby's right side, using your index and middle finger, walk your fingers across the tummy between the diaphragm and the navel from right to left using medium pressure. This helps to move gas and waste through the colon. Also, placing your baby on his or her left side allows gravity to assist with digestion.

_____

_____

_____

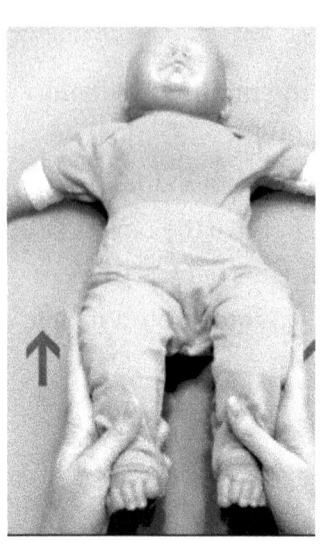 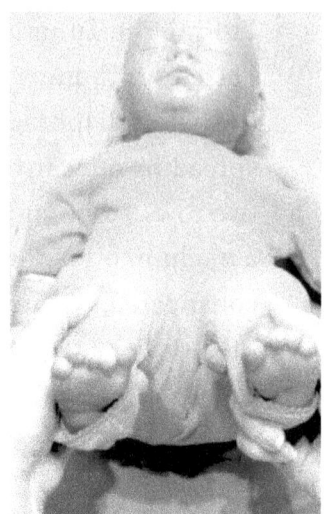

5. Knee to Tummy Press: Supporting the ankles and knees, gently press the legs into the tummy and hold for three to five seconds. This is your baby's natural way of passing gas or moving waste.

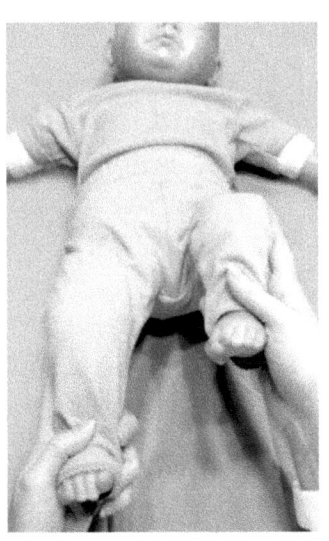 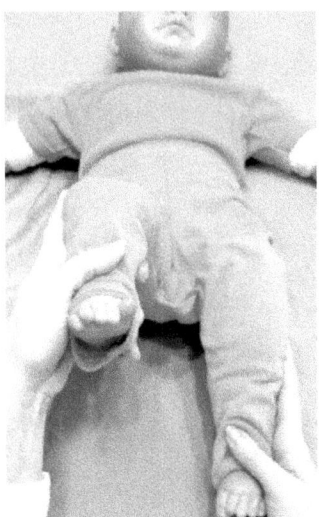

6. **Bicycle:** Supporting the ankles and knees, gently bend one knee up to the abdomen and bring it back down. Then alternate with the other leg. Repeat the bicycle motion slowly and rhythmically a few times. This can help your baby pass gas.

The Tummy Massage can be repeated throughout the day as needed. Typically, the tummy should be soft like a pillow. If tummy feels hard or tight, your baby is gassy or needs to potty, which may make the massage uncomfortable. You can always pick your baby up for burping after any portion of the tummy massage then proceed to the next step.

CHEST

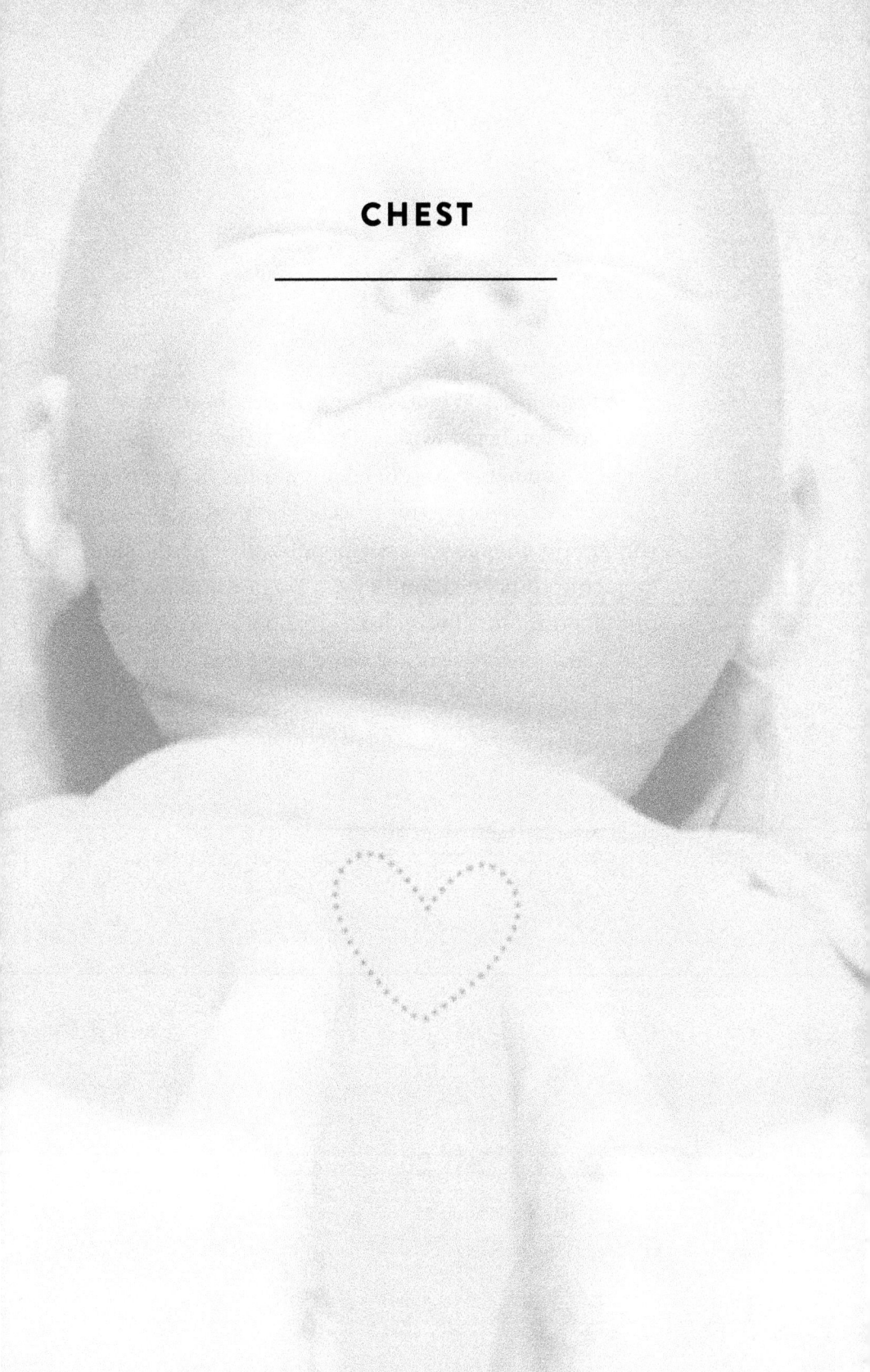

Getting started: When working on the chest, arms, or face, you begin working in your baby's intimate space. If you notice your baby not wanting to make eye contact with you or turning his or her head away from you, simply change your position. Work from the side or turn your baby around so you are not working in a frontal position. This is also a great bonding massage. Make lots of eye contact and say, "I love you."

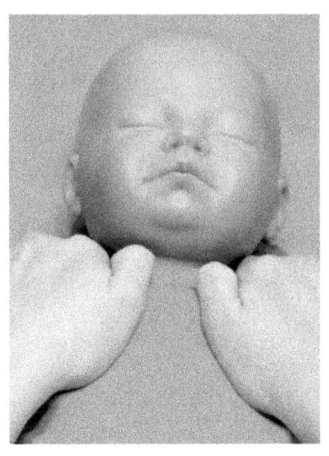

1. **Shoulder Press:**
   Gently cup your hands around your baby's shoulders. Looking into your baby's eyes, say, "Hello," and say your baby's name. This is a great bonding tool.

   _____

   _____

   _____

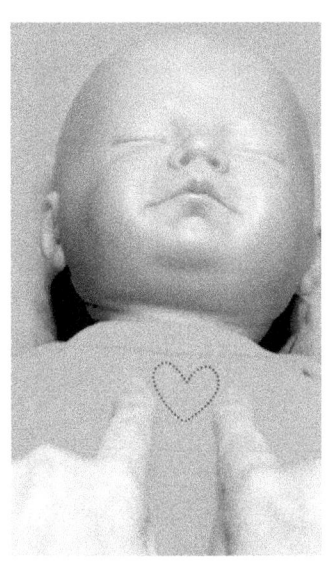

2. **Make a Heart Shape:**
   Using your index fingers, outline a small shape of a heart on the baby's sternum. Making good eye contact, say, "I love you," and your baby's name.

   Note: Make sure to keep the outline of the heart small. We want to teach our babies a healthy loving touch. As our children grow, both girls and boys, if they have experienced healthy touch all their lives, they will know when they are being touched inappropriately.

   _____

   _____

   _____

ARMS AND HANDS

Getting started: Arms and hand massage increases good circulation, so start with either the right or left arm. Do all the massage strokes on one arm, and then switch to the other arm and repeat the steps.

Repeat each massage stroke three times each.

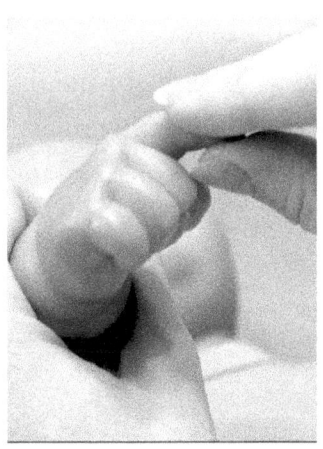

1. **Gently Massage Each Finger:**
   Support the hand at the wrist with one hand and then using the fingers of our other hand, gently massage and rotate through each finger using medium pressure, starting with the thumb.

   _____

   _____

   _____

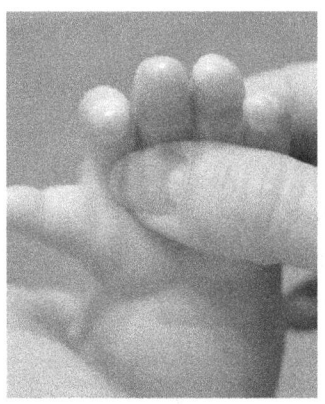

2. **Pressing Through the Palm of the Hand:**
   With your thumb, apply medium pressure and press below the fingers and all around the palm of the hand. You may also use circular massage on the palm of the hand.

   _____

   _____

   _____

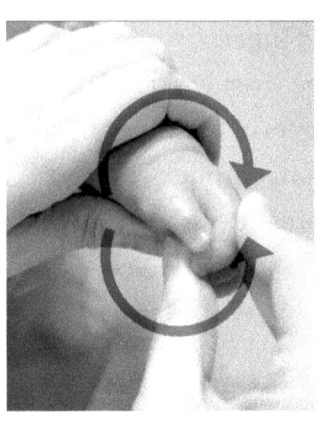

3. **Stretching of the Wrist:**
   Support the hand at the wrist with one hand and then using your other hand, gently rotate the wrist to the right three times. Then rotate the wrist to the left three times.

4. **Circular Massage on Top of the Hand:**
   Using both of your thumbs, do small, circular massage on top of the hand, using gentle to medium pressure. You can also use your thumb applying circular massage. This helps with circulation and blood flow.

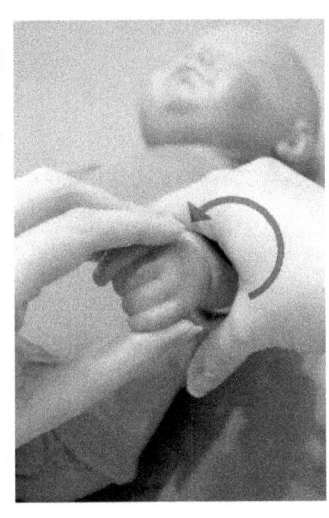

5. Effleurage to the Arms:

Effleurage is a gliding stroke, long and smooth. Support the wrist with one hand and then using the other hand, starting at the outside of the wrist, make a "C" shape with your hand. Using medium pressure, roll into the inner wrist, glide up the inner arm, glide out to the outer arm, and glide back down to the wrist.

Note: You can also knead the arm in a circular motion. Starting at the wrist and using medium pressure, begin kneading (like dough) up the arm and glide back down the arm.

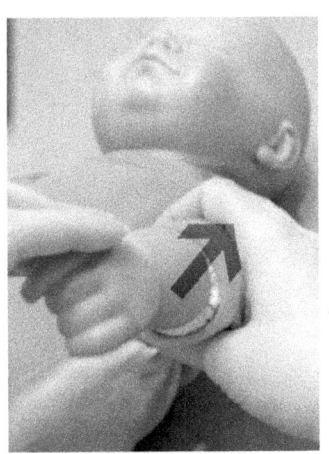
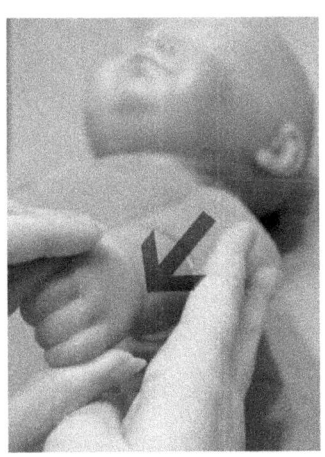

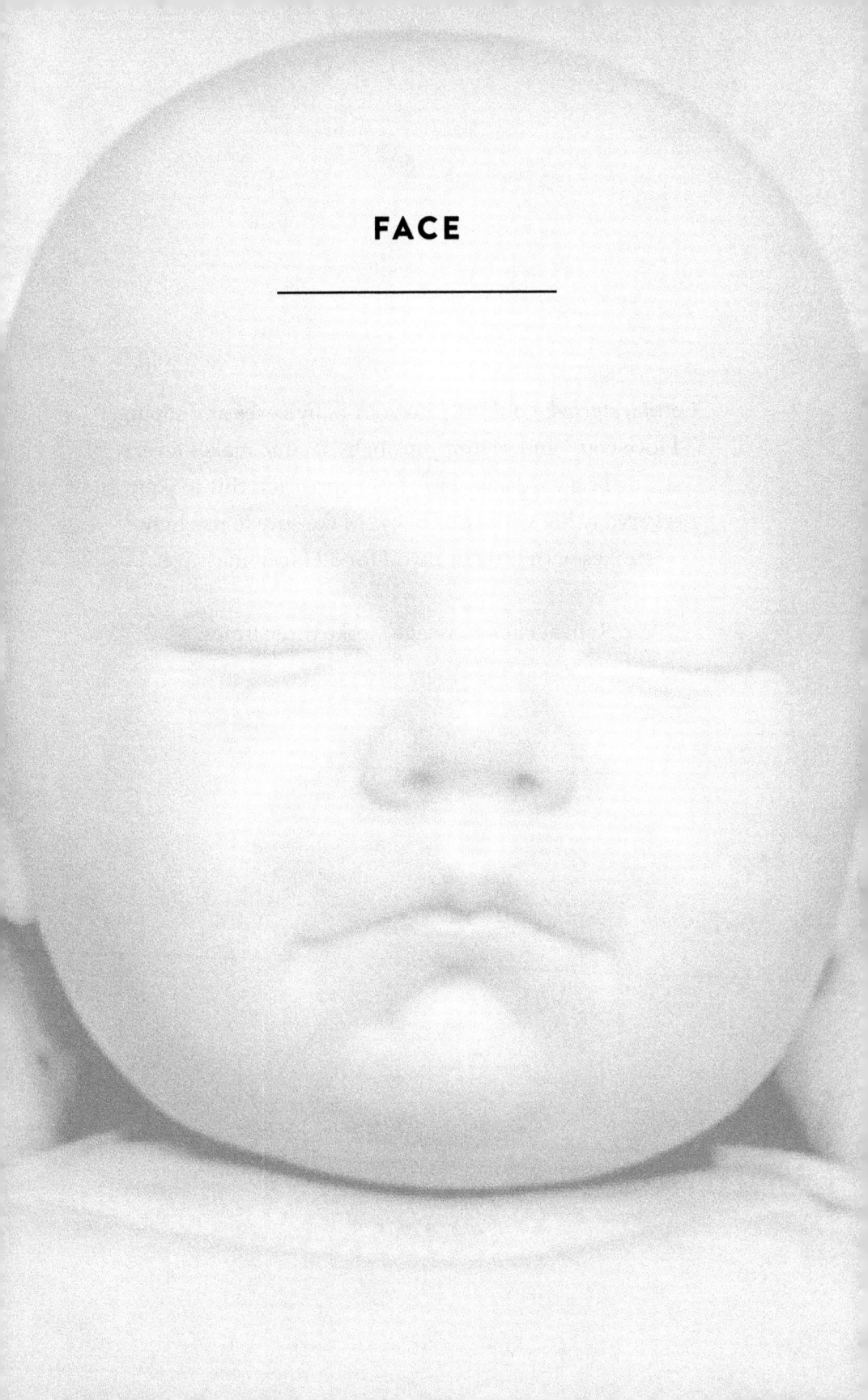

FACE

Getting started: Looking into your baby's eyes and saying, "I love you," and saying your baby's name makes a very strong bond. Always look for ways to add this to your everyday life with your baby. Make sure to use light strokes with little or no oil for all facial massage.

Repeat each massage stroke three times.

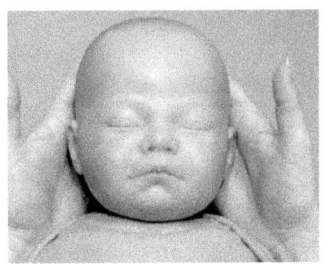

1. **Holding Your Baby's Head:**

   Hold your baby's head gently in your hands. Making good eye contact say, "I love you," and say your baby's name.

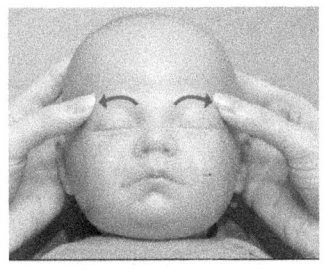

2. **Sweeping Over the Eyebrows:**

   Using your thumbs, gently and with featherlike pressure, sweep over your baby's eyebrows. You can gently sweep over the forehead, up to the hairline, and back down the eyebrows.

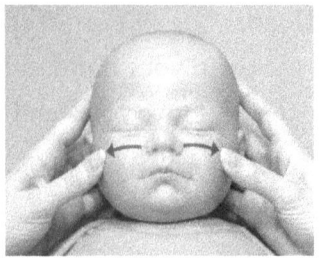

3. Sweeping Over the Cheeks:
Using your thumbs with gentle featherlike pressure, sweep across the cheeks to the outer edge of the face. You can also apply gentle circular massage across the cheeks using your thumbs.

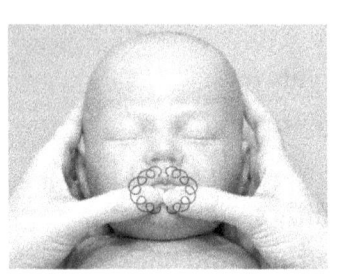

4. Circular Massage Around the Mouth:
Using your index fingers, make small gentle, circular massage motions around the outside of the mouth.

Note: Start this massage technique when your baby is an infant, and when your baby starts teething, he or she may allow you to massage around the mouth, which will increase blood flow and oxygen, therefore relieving pain. You can even purchase a finger-toothbrush massager. Place this on your index finger and do circular massage inside the baby's mouth over baby's gums. This too will help with teething.

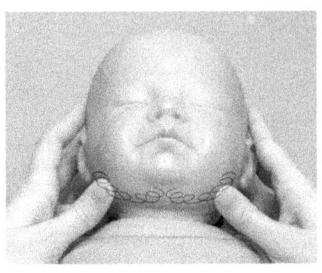

5. Sweeping Under the Chin:

Using your thumbs, gently sweep along the jawline. You can also apply gentle circular massage along the jawline using your thumbs.

_____

_____

_____

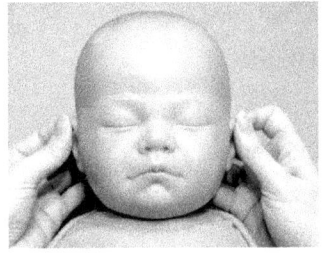

6. Massage the Ears:

Using your thumbs and index fingers, gently lift the ears and apply circular massage around the outer edges of the ears.

_____

_____

_____

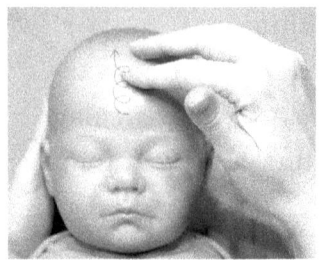

7. Circular Scalp Massage:

Using your fingertips, gently apply circular massage all over your baby's head.

Note: Be EXTRA careful around the soft spot on the baby's head. Use very gentle pressure.

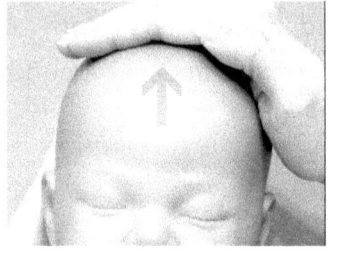

8. Sweeping the Baby's Head:

Using the palm of your hand, starting from the forehead, make a gentle featherlike sweep over the entire head to the neckline. Babies LOVE this!

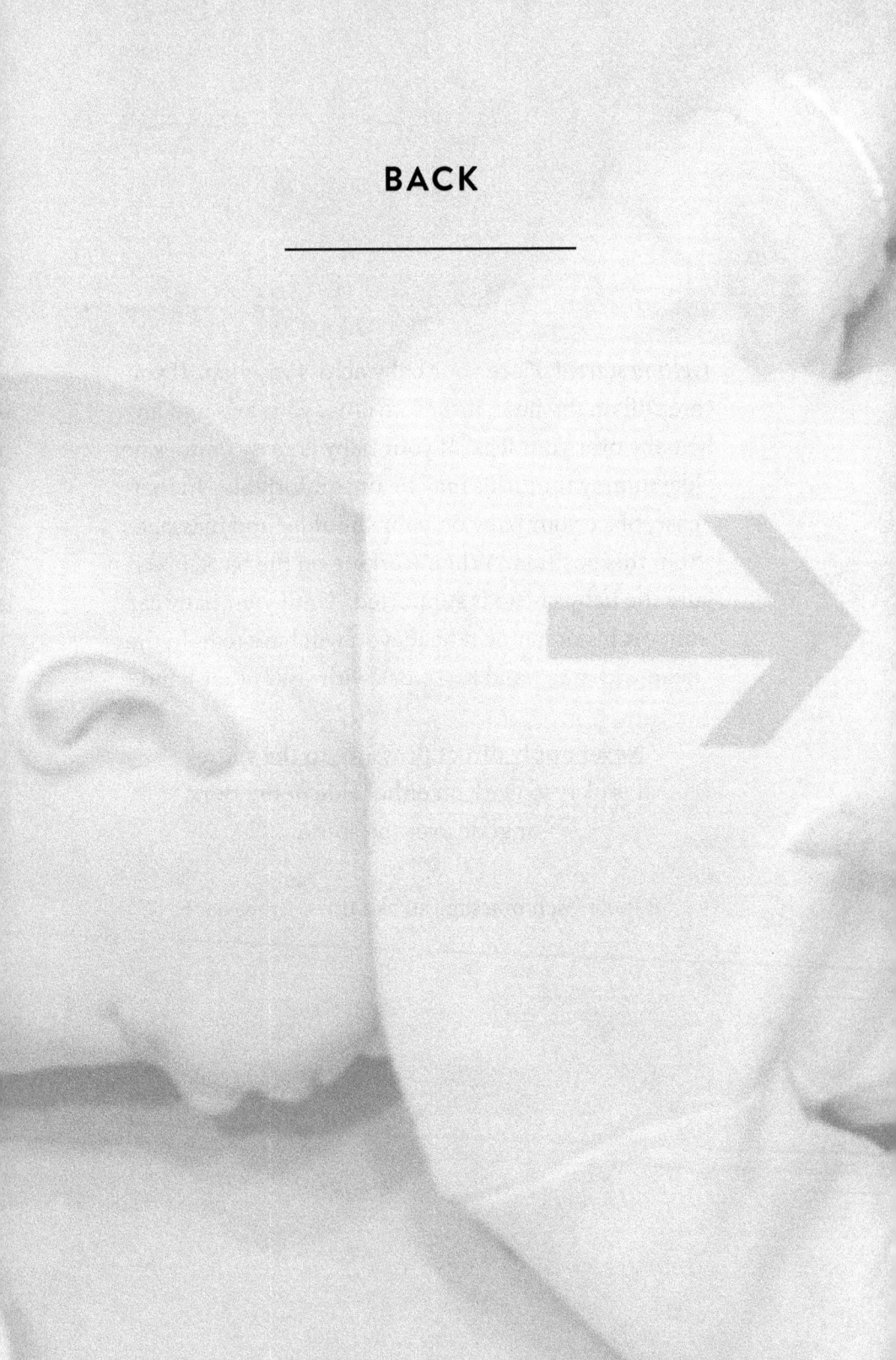

BACK

Getting started: Place your baby across your lap. If you are still on the floor, its best to cross your legs and lay the baby over your legs. If your baby is gassy or does not like tummy time, this may be uncomfortable. In that case, place your baby on your shoulder and massage from this position. When working on the back, make sure the baby's head is supported. Until your baby can support his or her own head, you will have to hold the head with one hand and work with your other hand.

<u>Never apply direct pressure to the spine!</u>
It is okay to work on either side of the spine
or glide over the spine.

Repeat each massage stroke three times each.

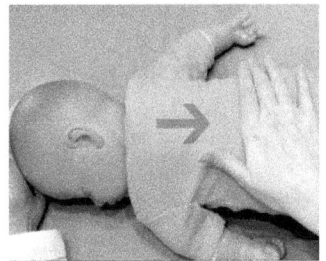

1. **Gliding Down the Back:**

   With the palm of your hand, start at your baby's neckline and use a gentle featherlike sweeping motion as you glide down the back stopping just at the hips.

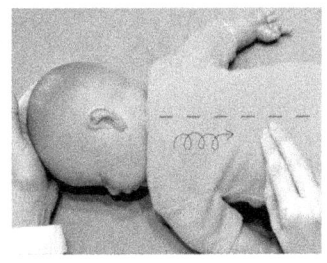

2. **Circular Massage:**

   Using your fingertips, apply gentle circular massage starting at the neckline and moving down one side of the spine and stopping just at the hips. Now using your fingertips, glide back up to the neckline.

   Repeat this three times one side of the spine.

   Then, switch to the other side of the spine and repeat three times on this side of the spine.

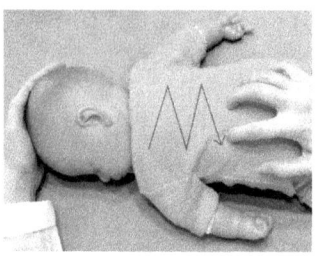

3. Zigzag Down the Back:

Using your fingertips and starting at the neckline, gently zigzag down the back stopping just at the hips.

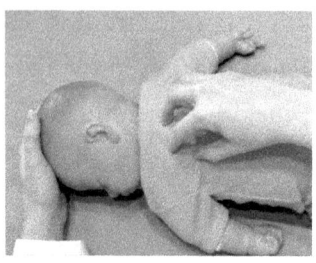

4. Scratching the Back:

Using your fingertips, gently scratch the baby's back, starting at the neckline and working down the back stopping at the hips. If you enjoy having your back scratched, I promise your baby will like it as much as you do.

CONCLUSION

You have completed the full-body infant massage!

Now, pick up your baby and give him or her a hug and a kiss. Saying your baby's name and make eye contact with them say, "You did a great job!" "I love you!"

I hope this step-by-step infant massage guide brings much love and joy to you and your baby.

Remember, even though this guide is laid out in an infant format, you can continue to offer massage as your child grows. This deepens the loving, secure, bond that is created during each massage.

www.ingramcontent.com/pod-product-compliance
Lightning Source LLC
Chambersburg PA
CBHW071316110426
42743CB00042B/2686